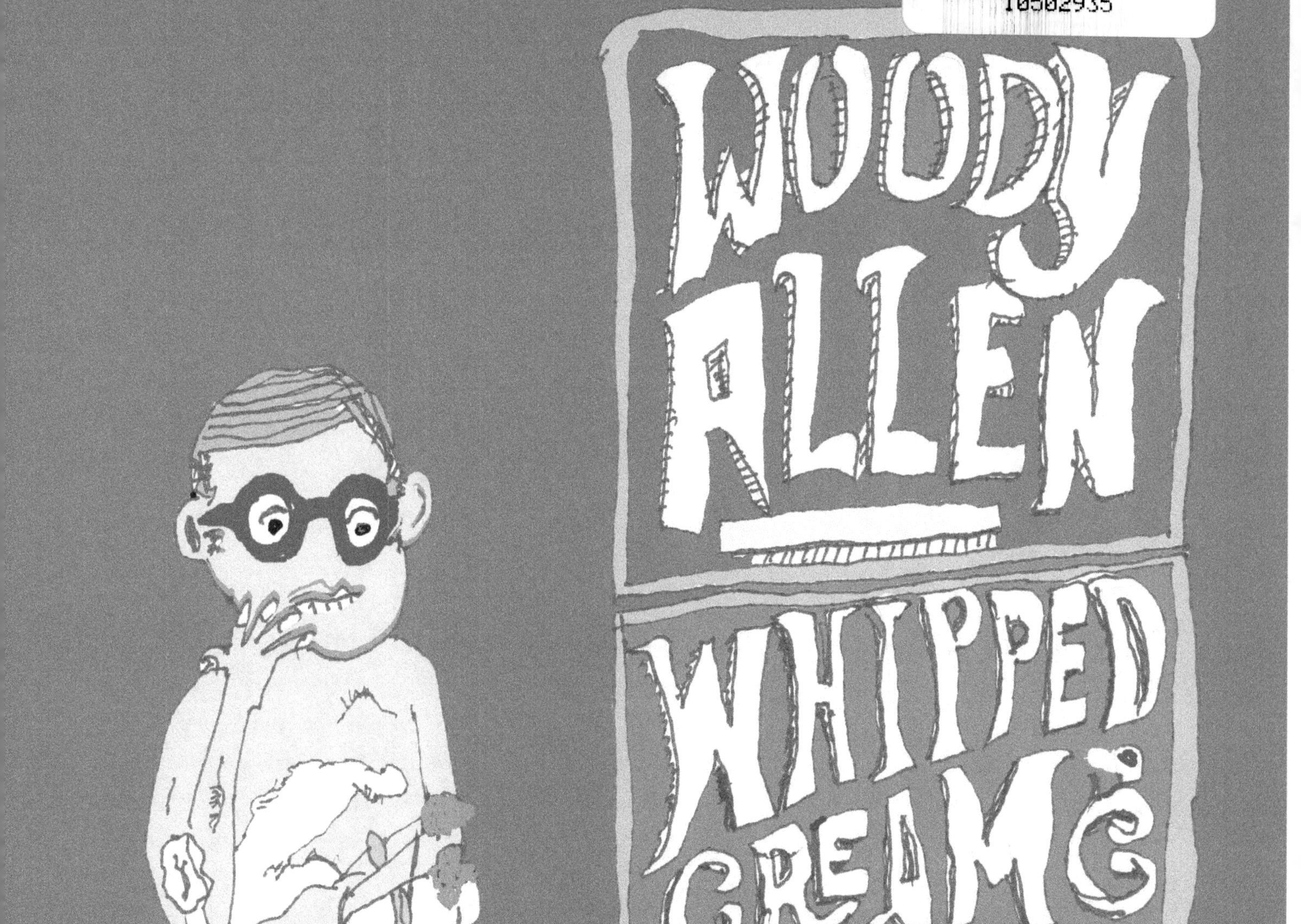

WOODY ALLEN

WHIPPED CREAM & OTHER DELIGHTS

DRAWINGS BY JOHN RIEGERT

Woody Allen Whipped Cream and Othr Delights © 2016 by John
Riegert

First Edition First Printing

http://www.johnriegert.com
john@johnriegert.com

ISBN: 978-1-365-49990-6

How this book came about:

I am an artist and I try to draw every day. Sometimes when I hit an "artist block"... just like a writer's block...I would do a simple exercise where I would find a picture of a women in a bathing suit and then I would visualize Woody Allen's face on it and then draw it. Usually that was all that was needed to get the creative juices flowing. Put Woody Allen in a bikini and there is an explosion.

Why Woody Allen?
Because it is funny.

Enjoy
- John Riegert

My one regret in life is
that I am not someone else.
- Woody Allen

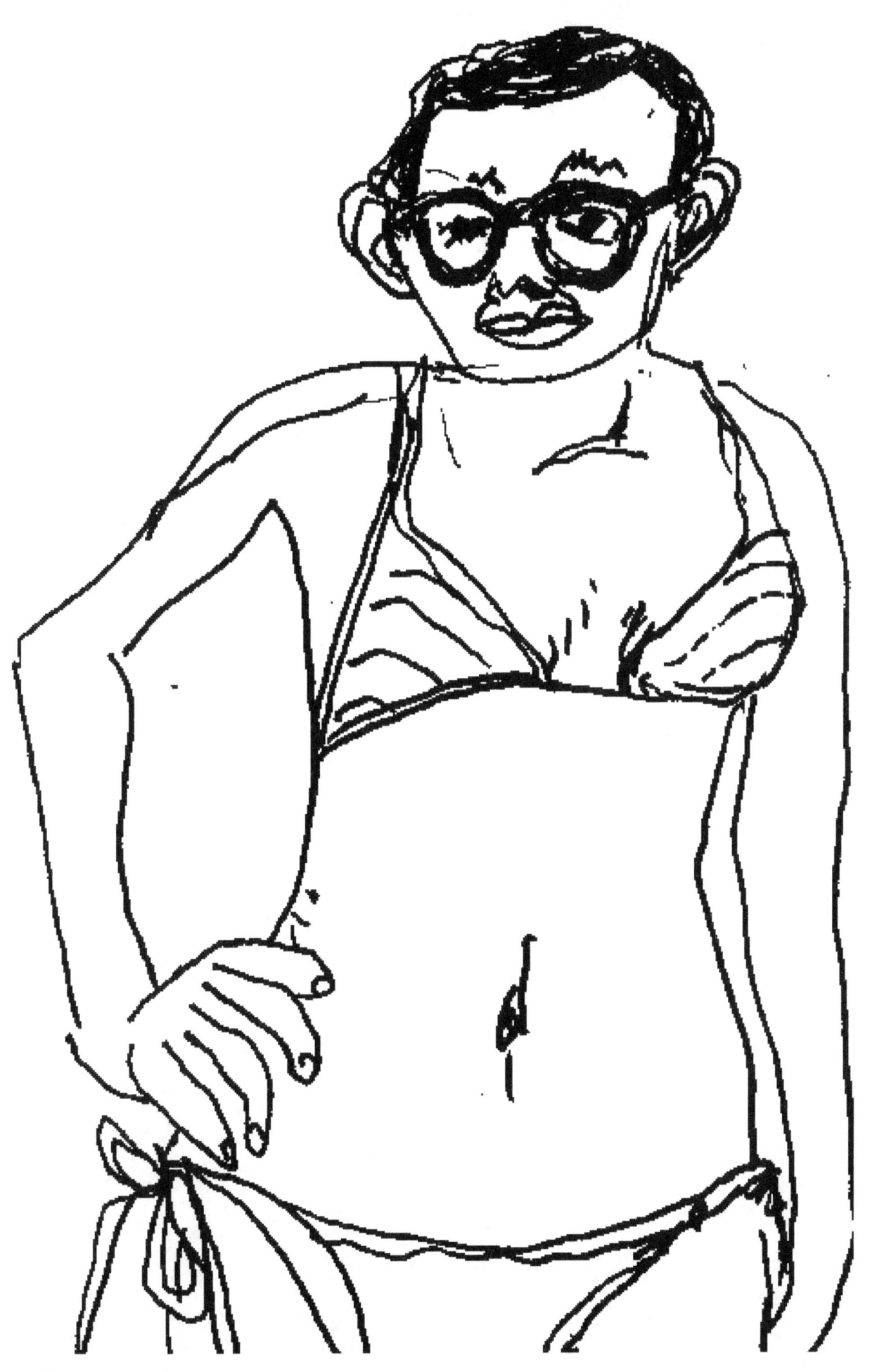

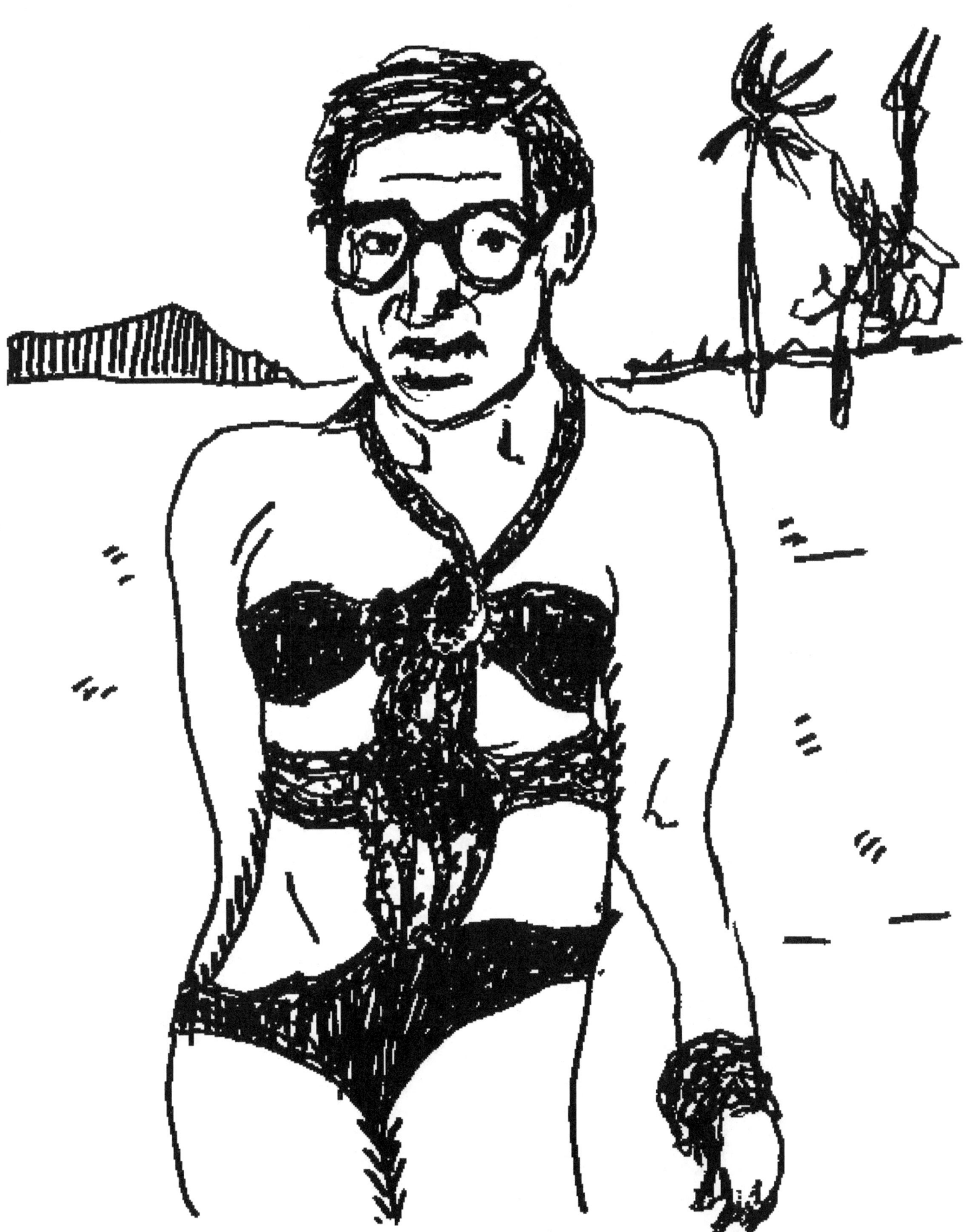

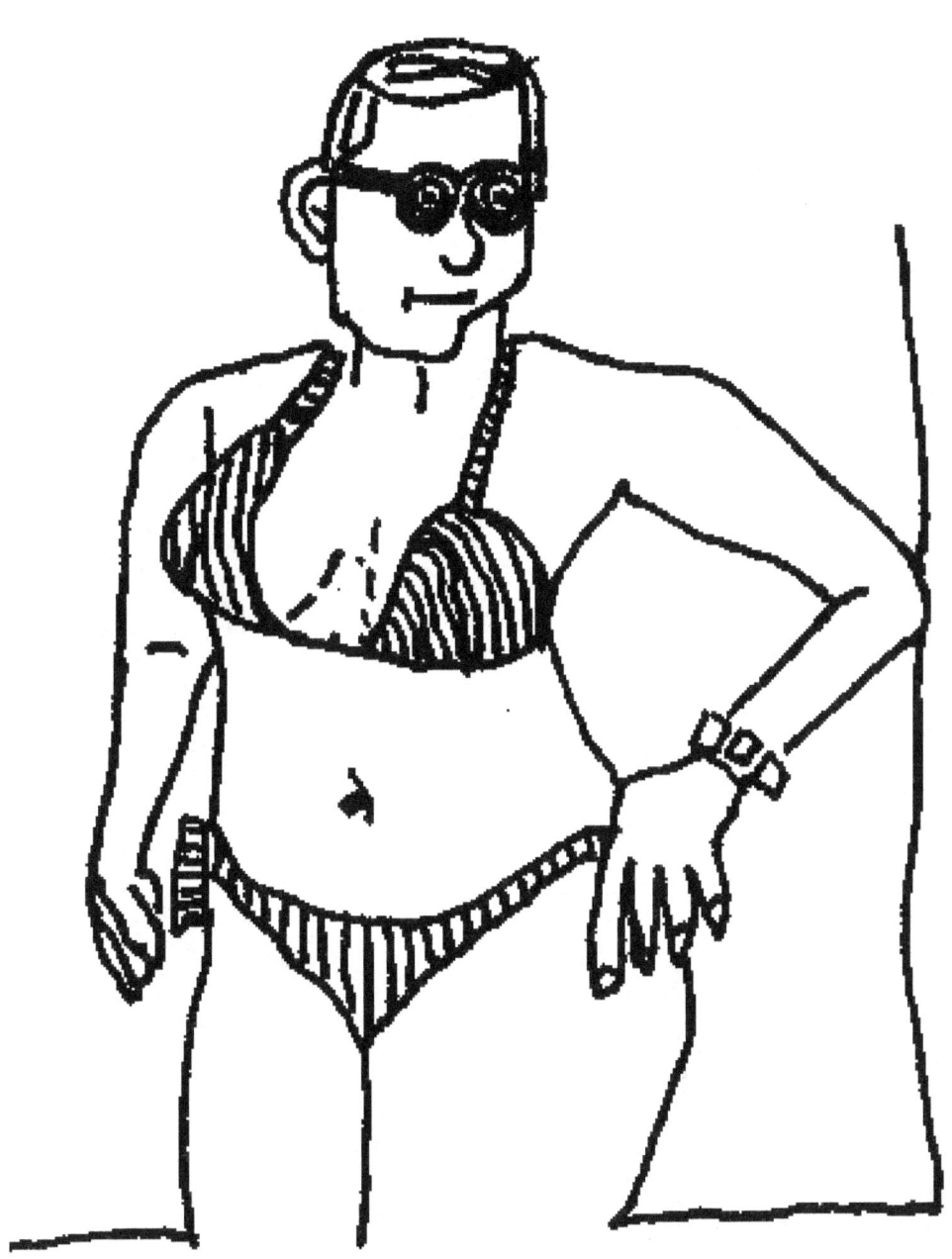

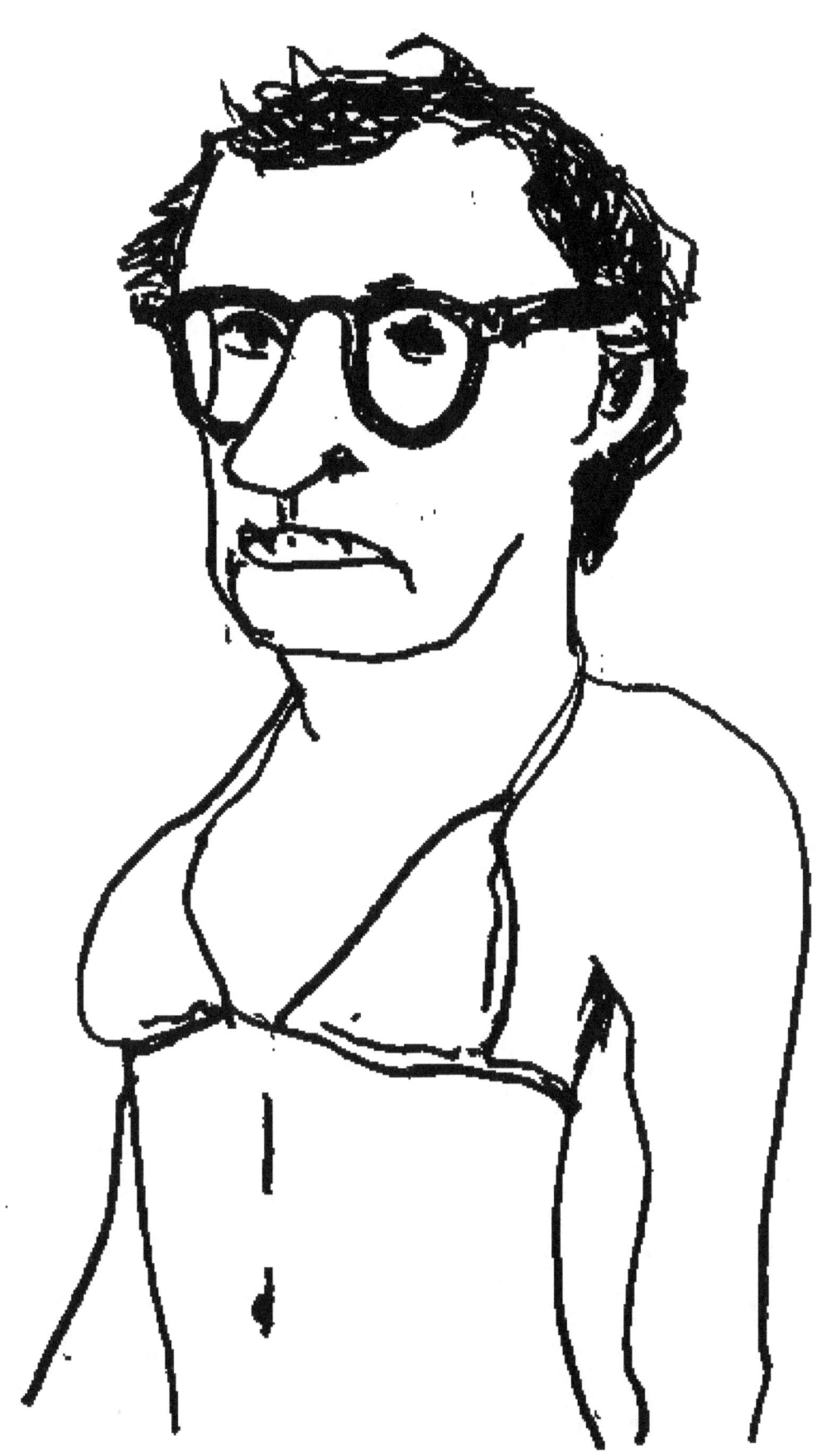

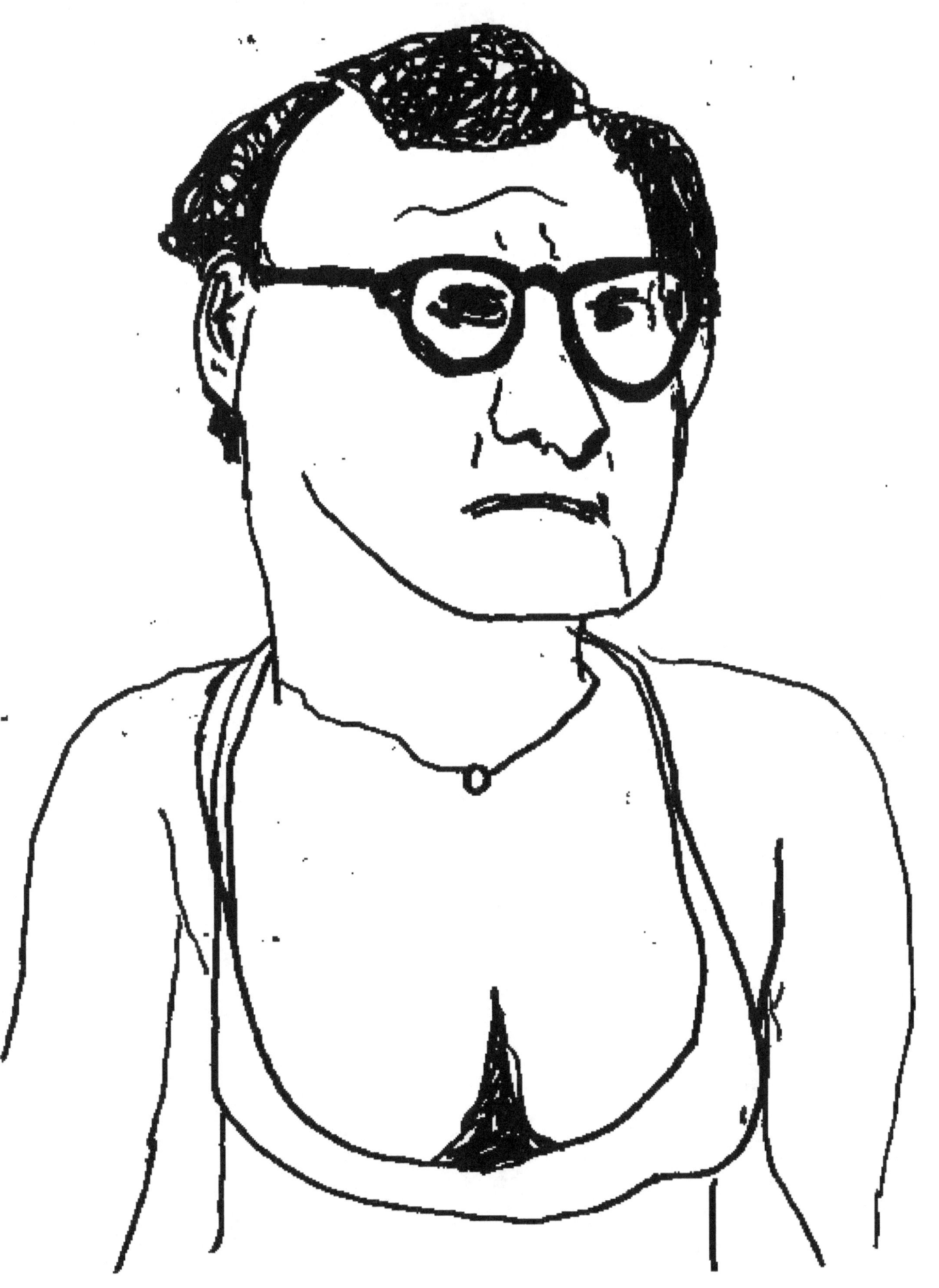

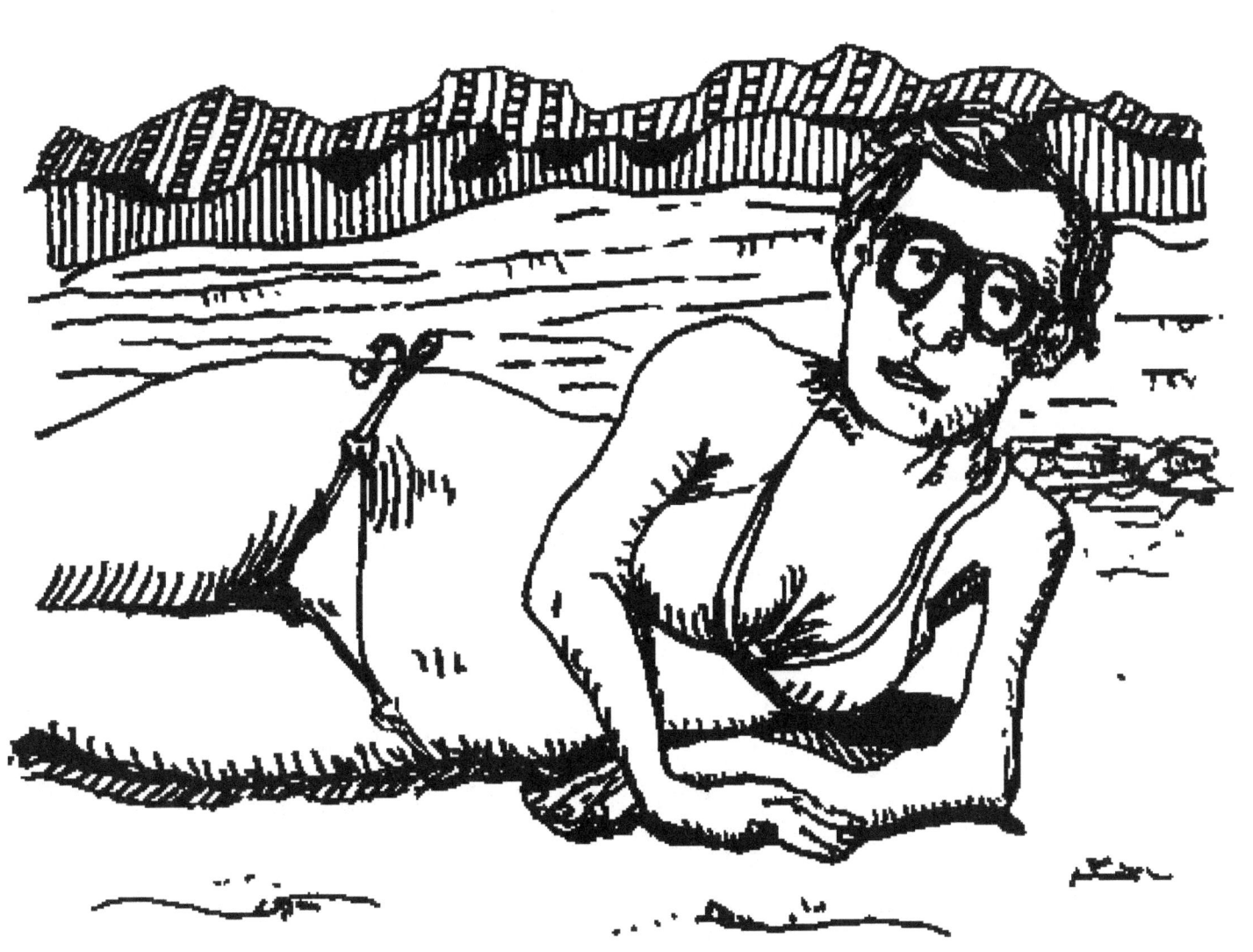

1.30.15
John

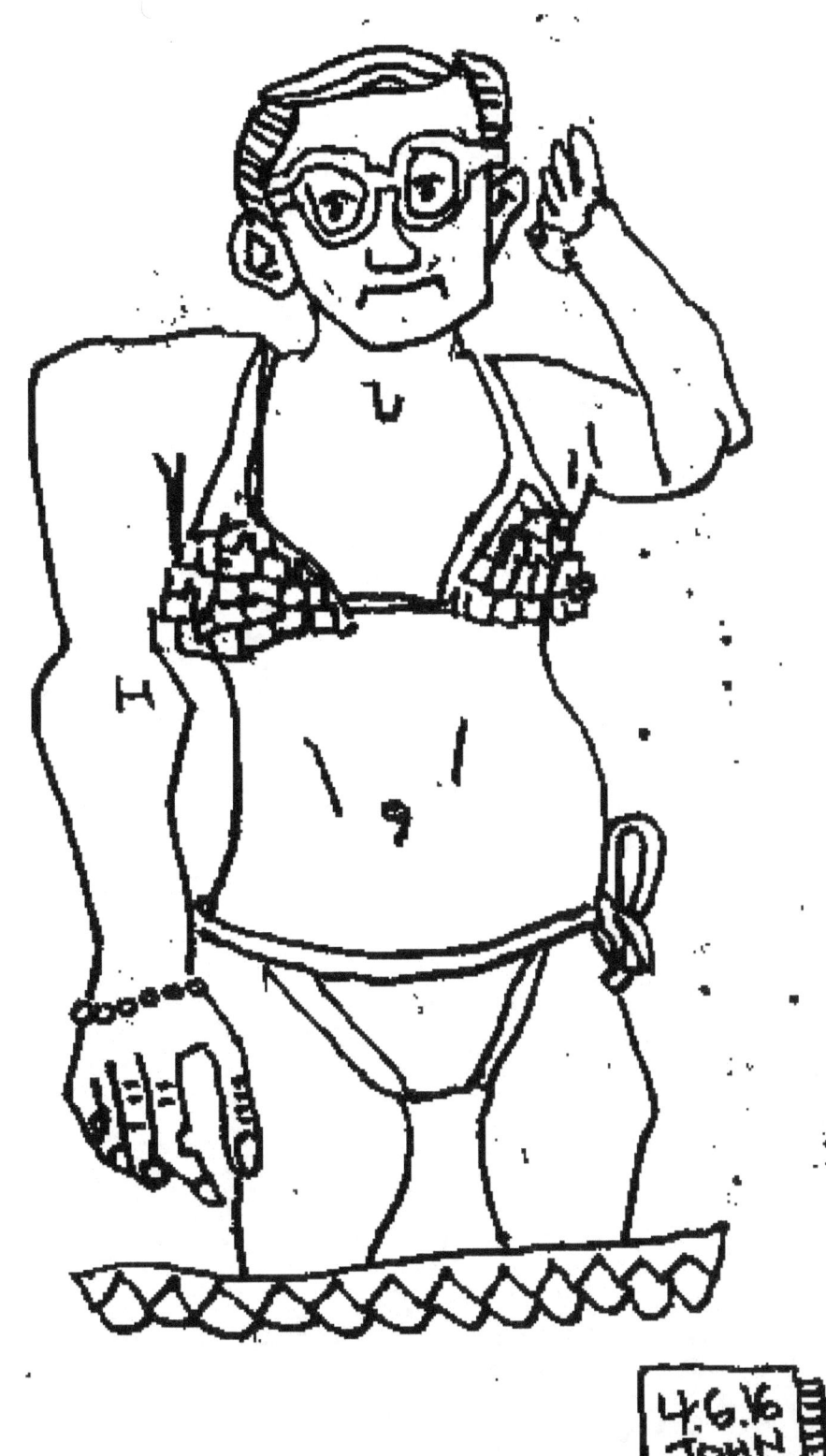

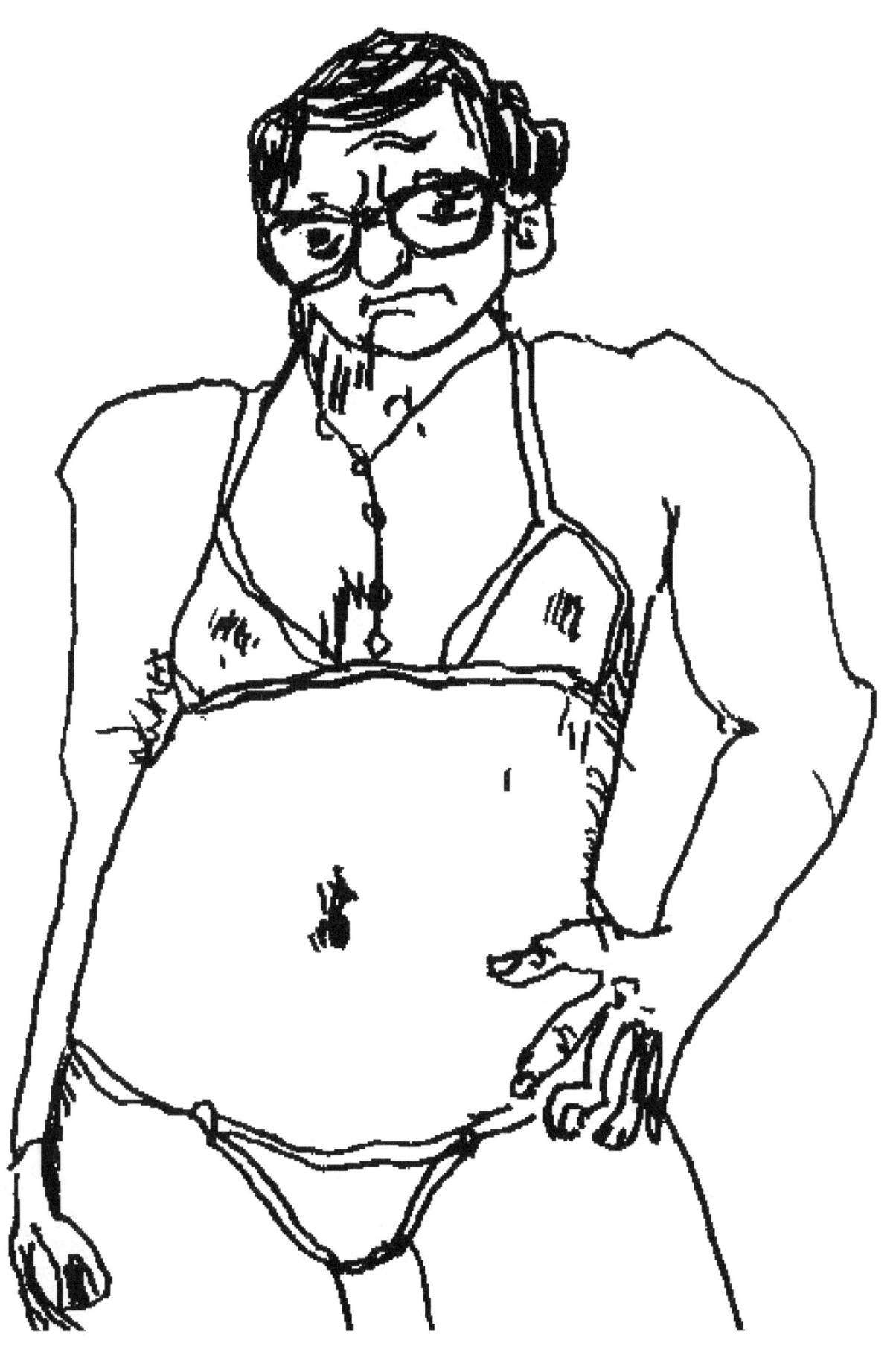

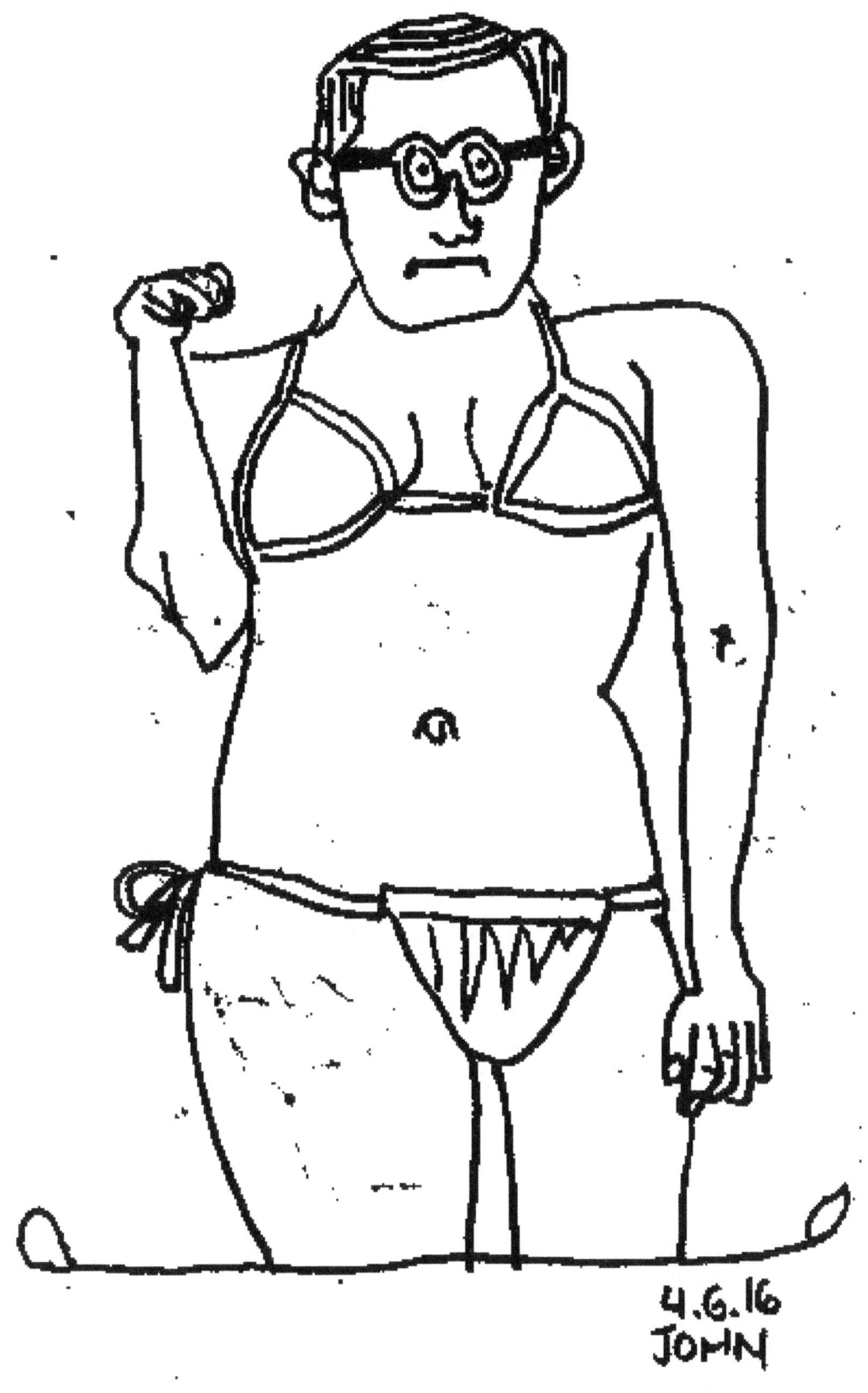

4.6.16
JOHN

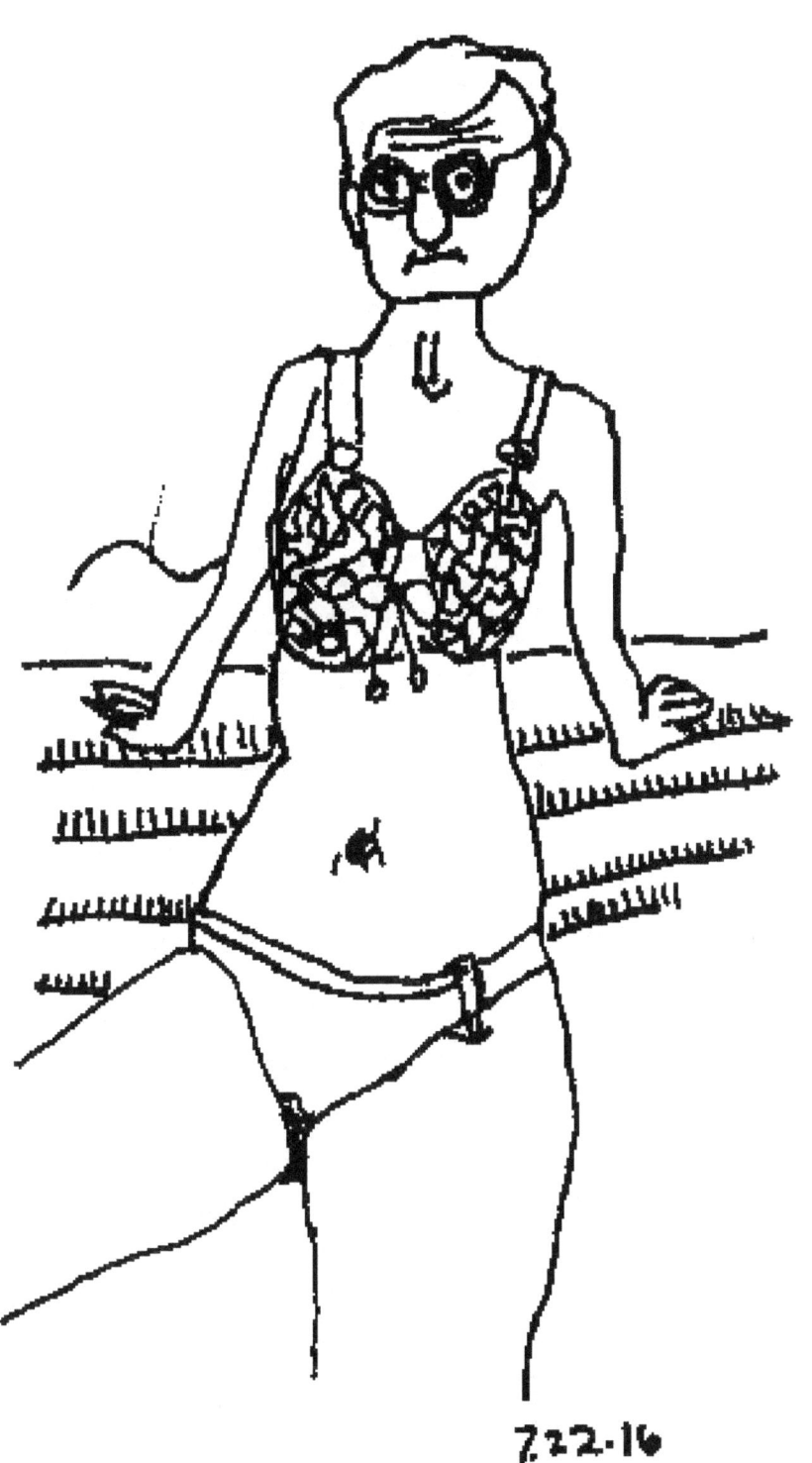

7.22.16

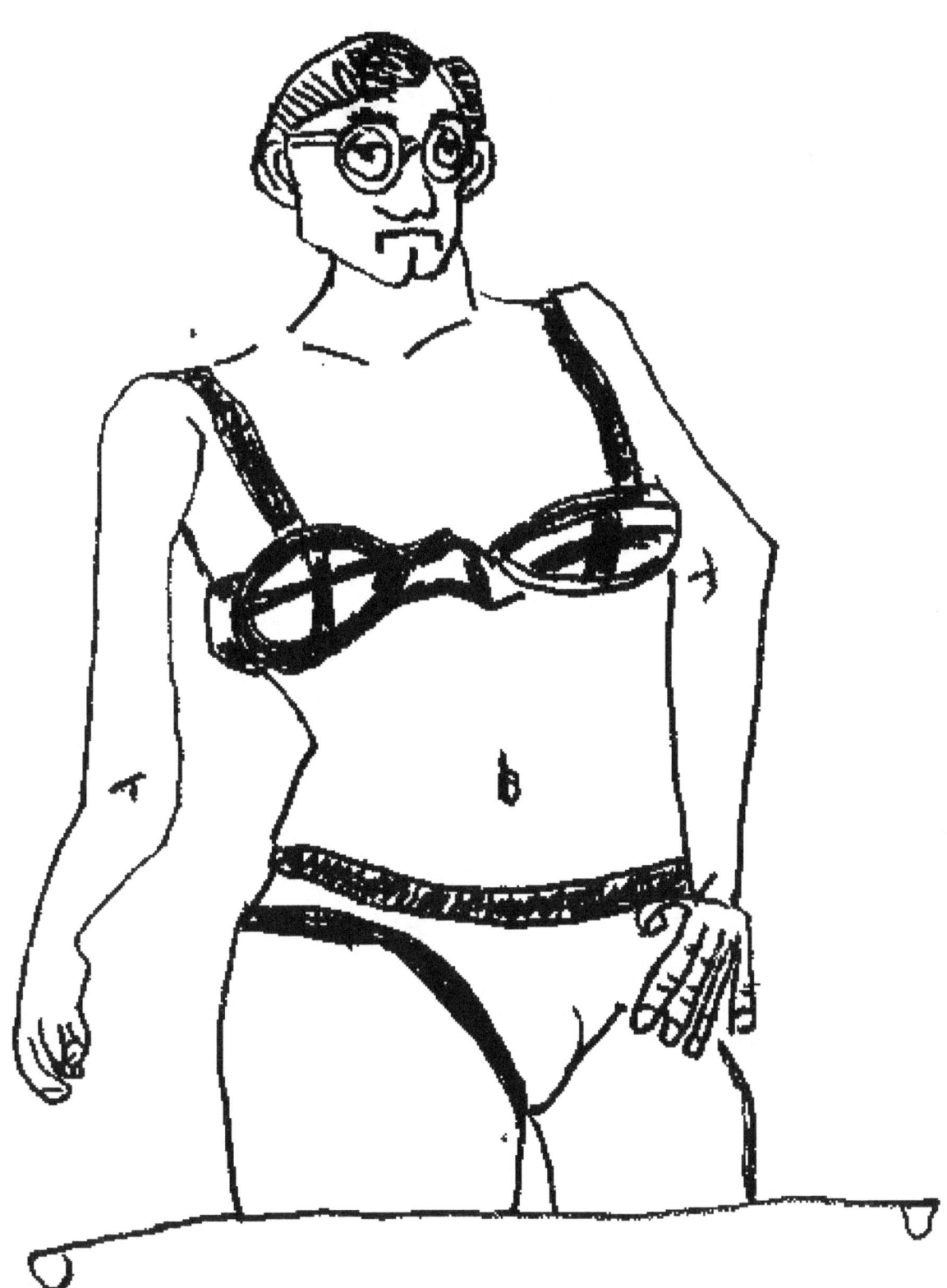

JOHN
4-14-16

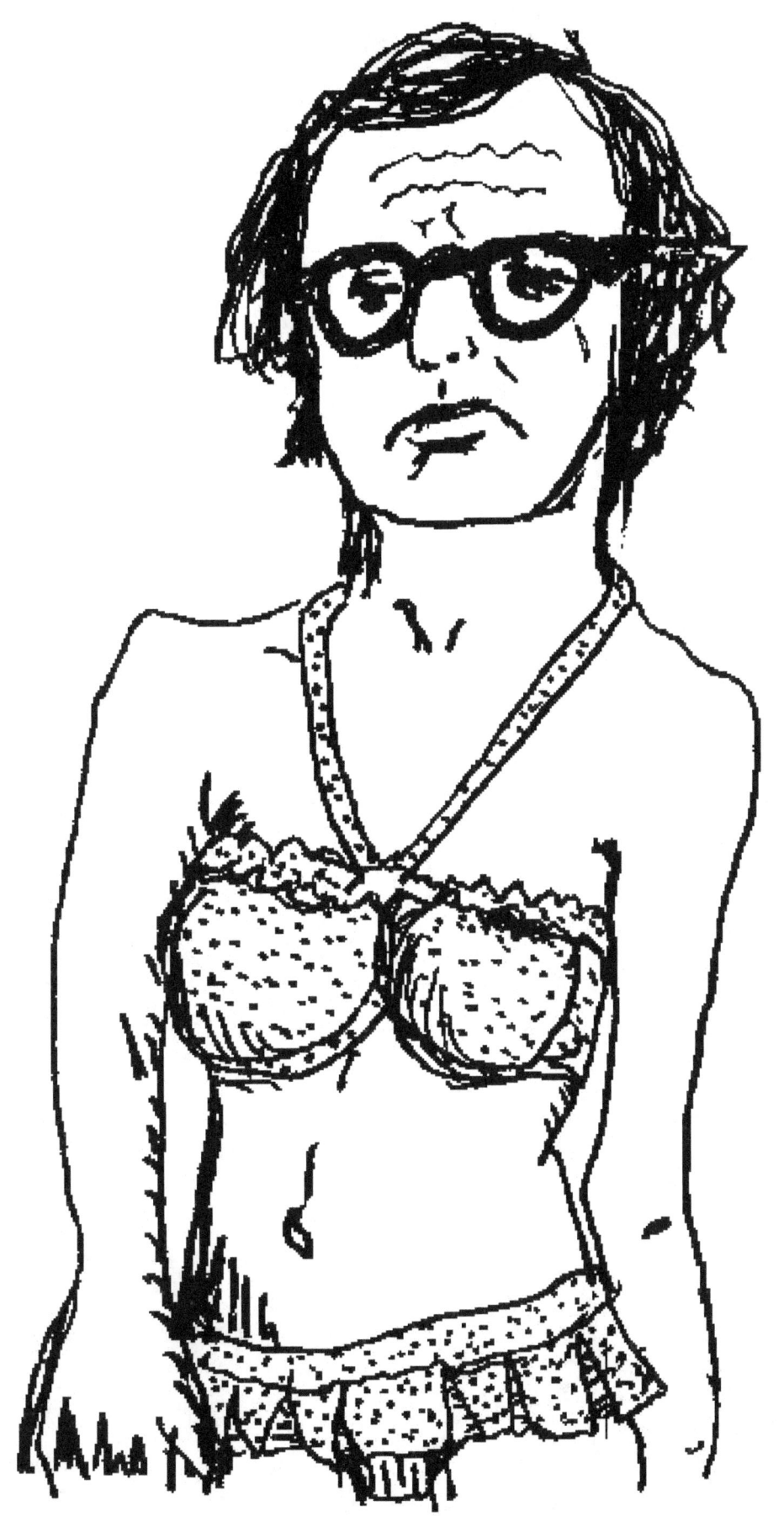

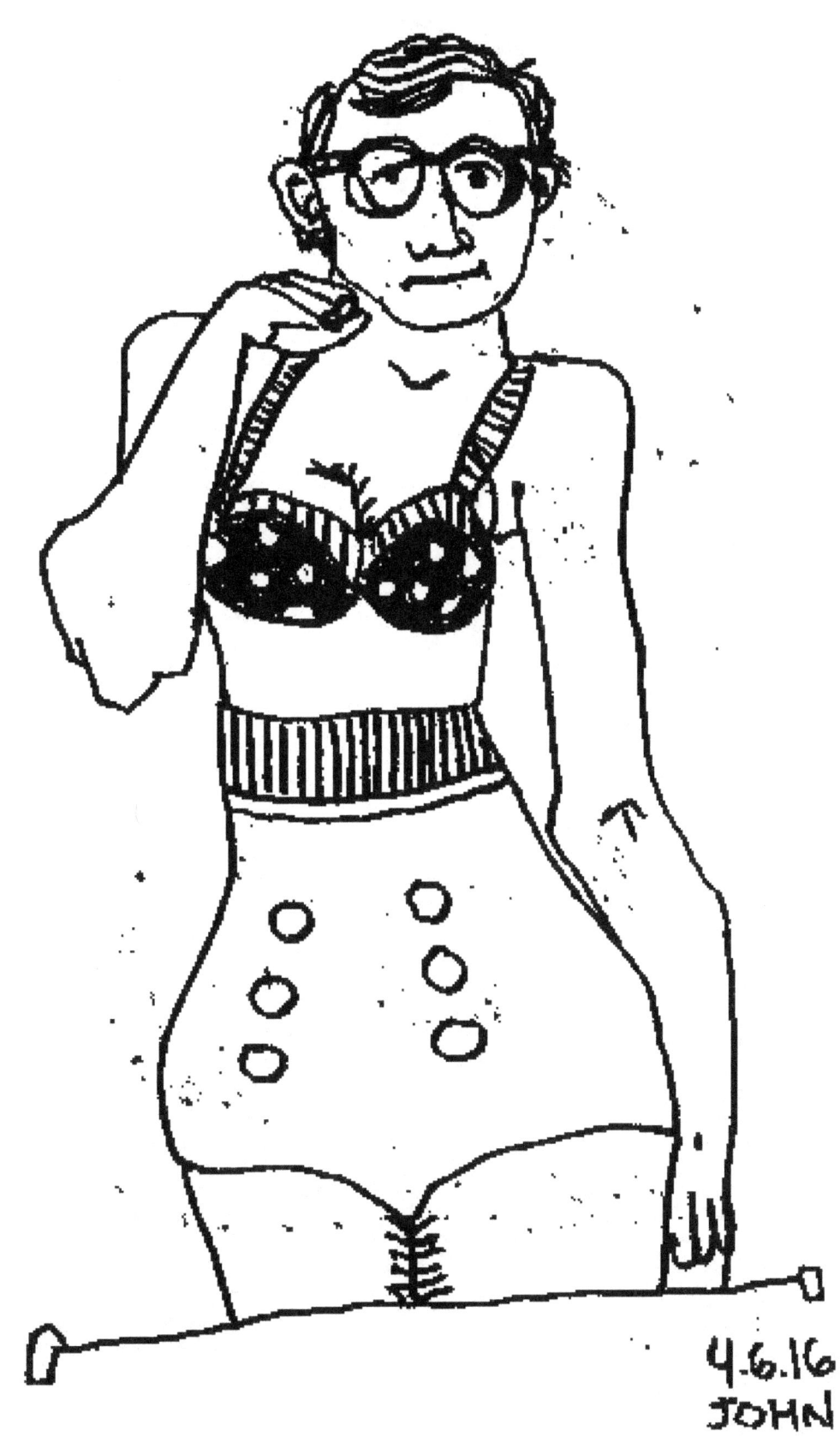

4.6.16
JOHN

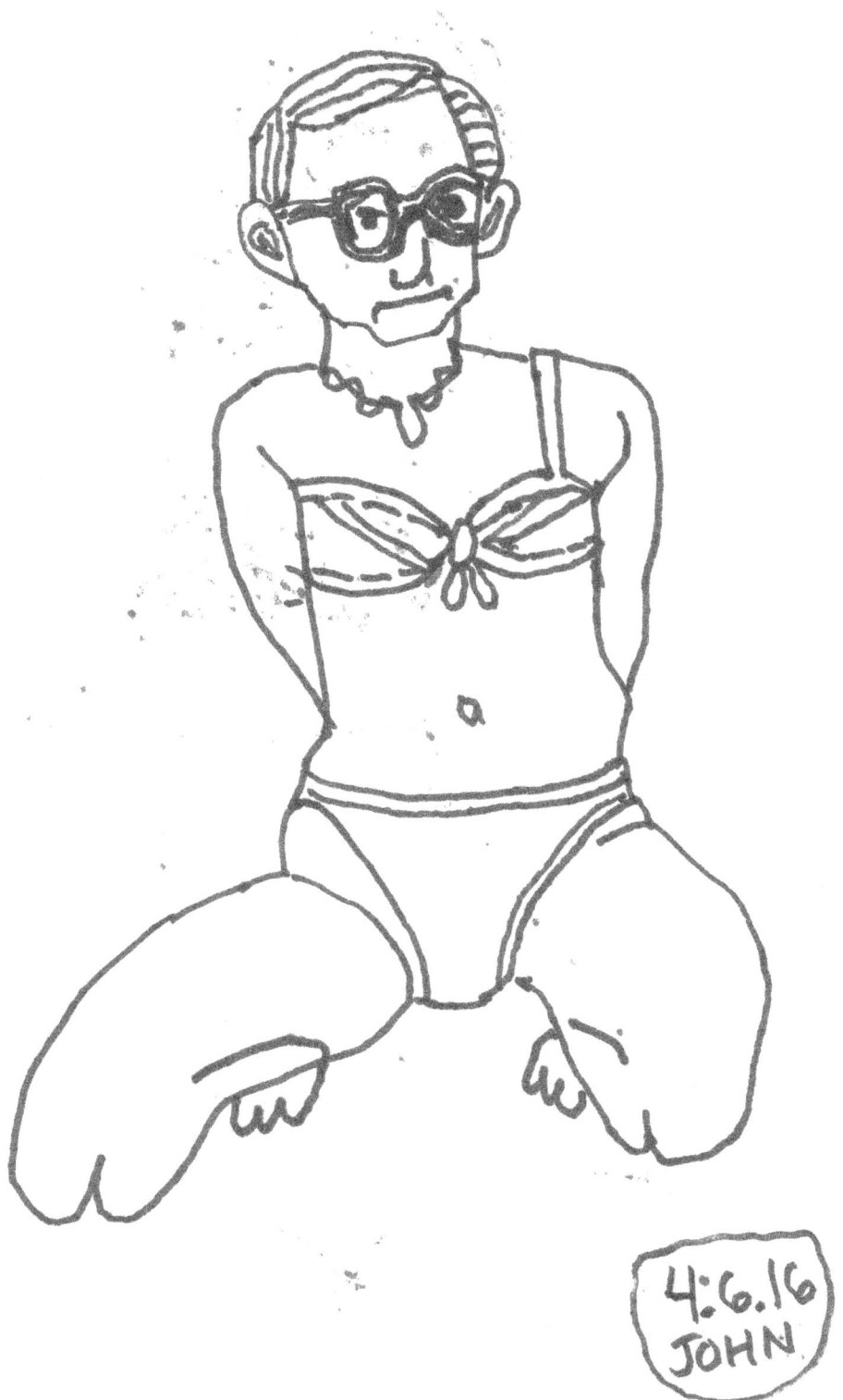

4:6.16
JOHN.

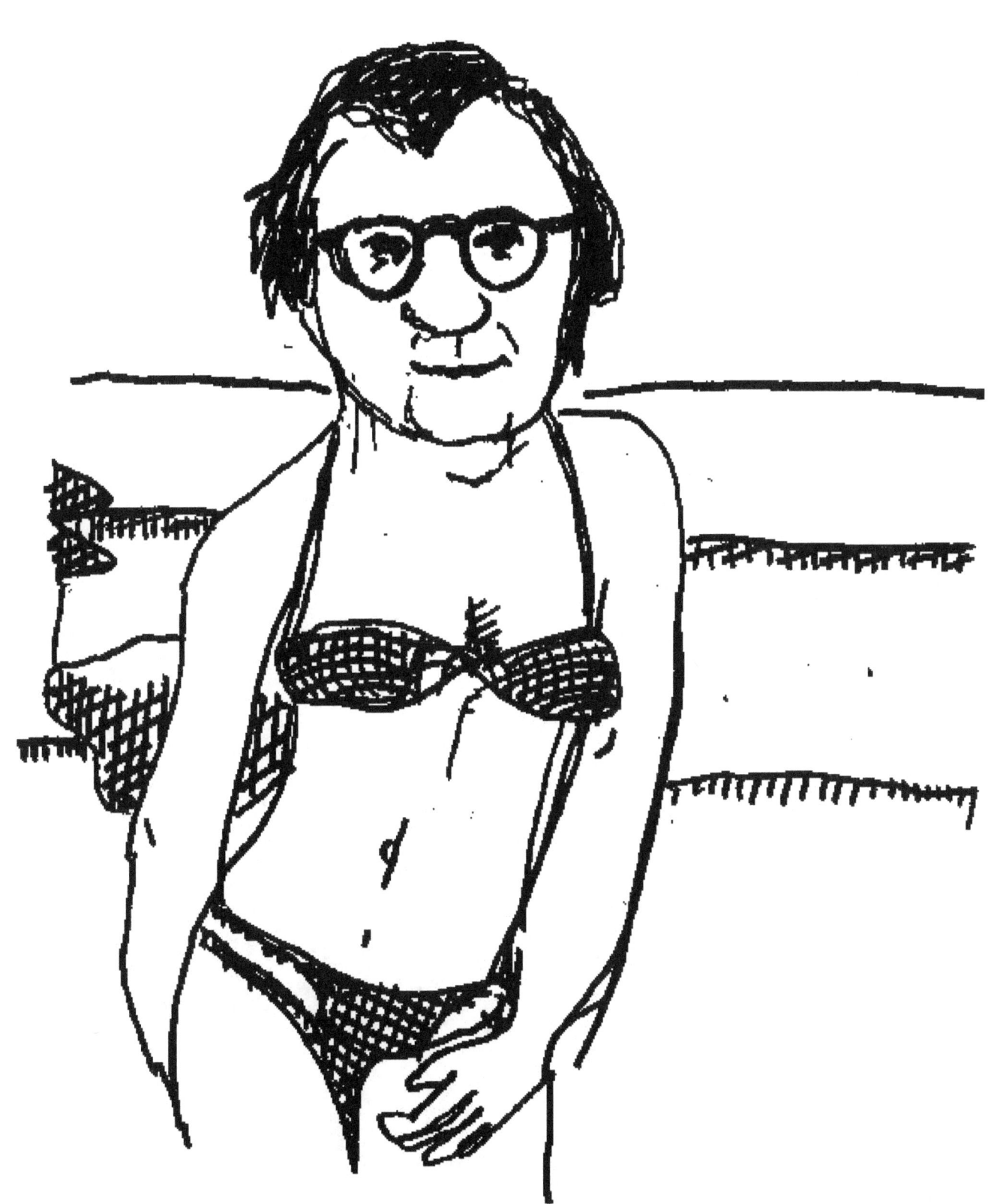

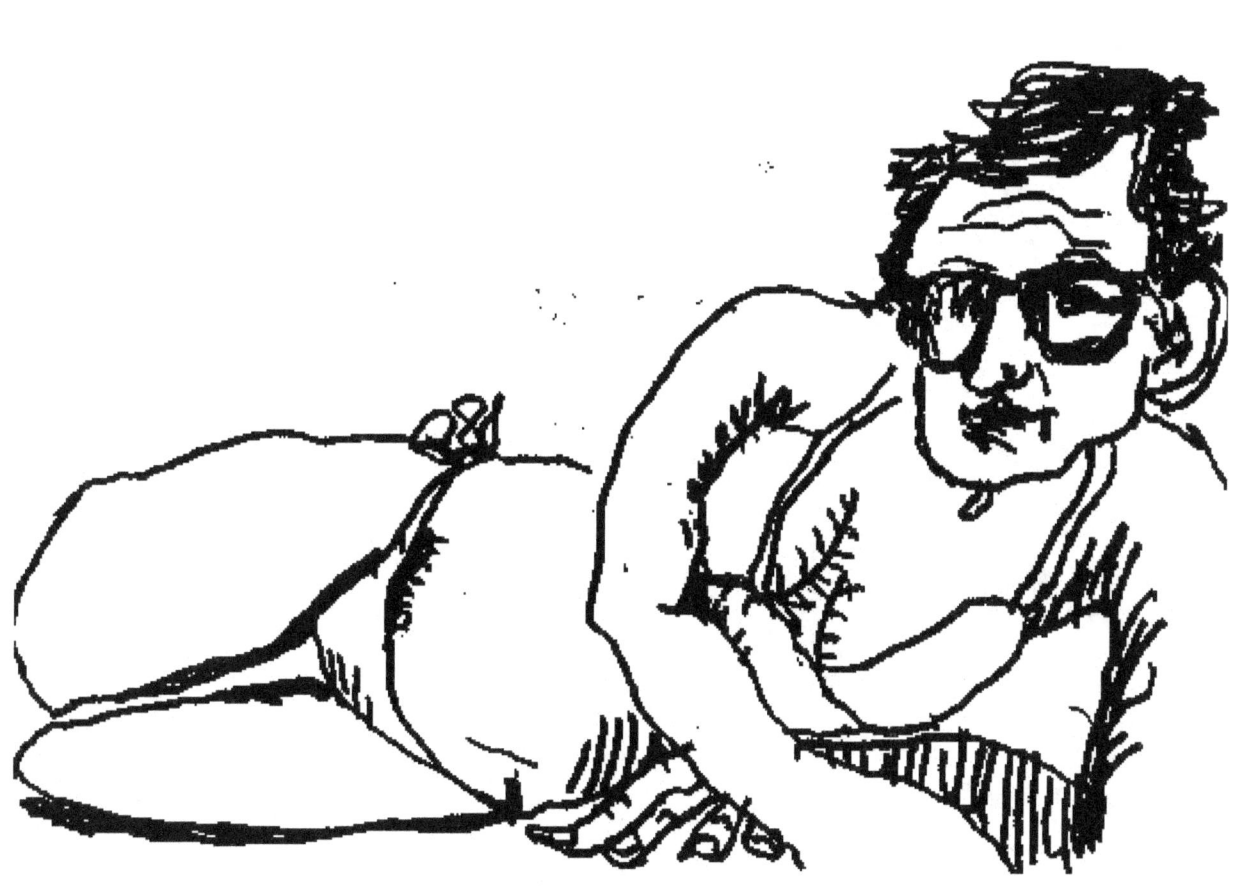

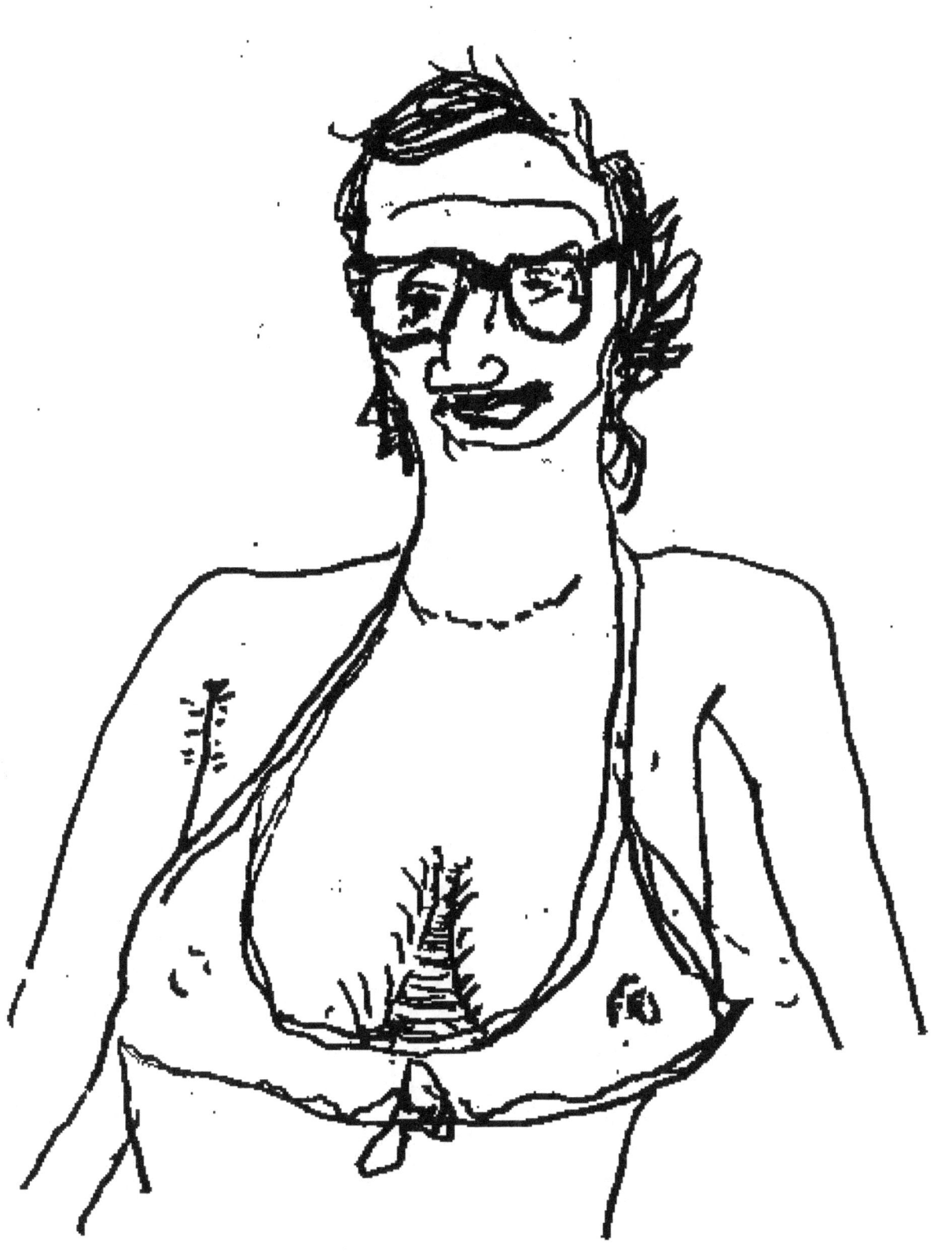

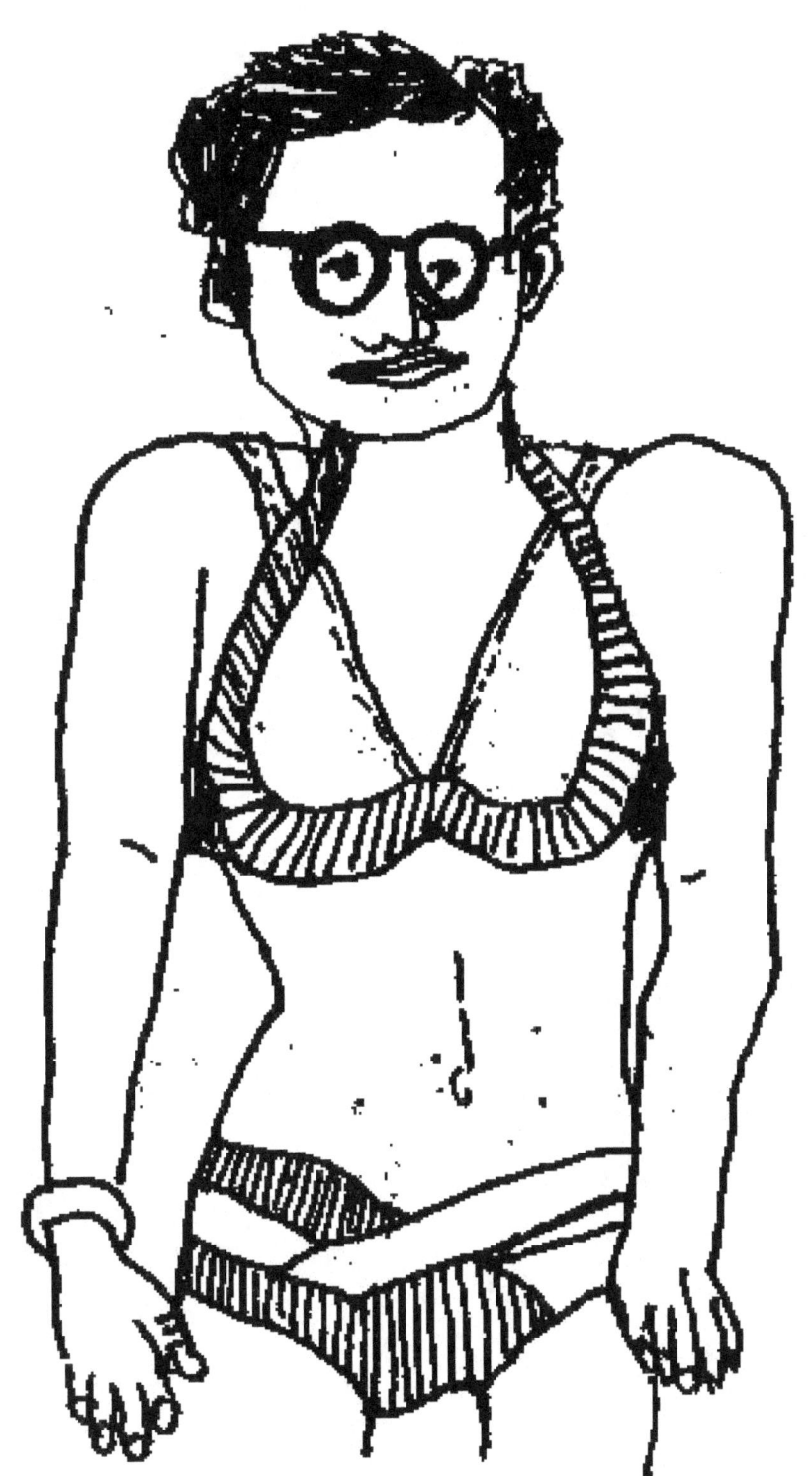

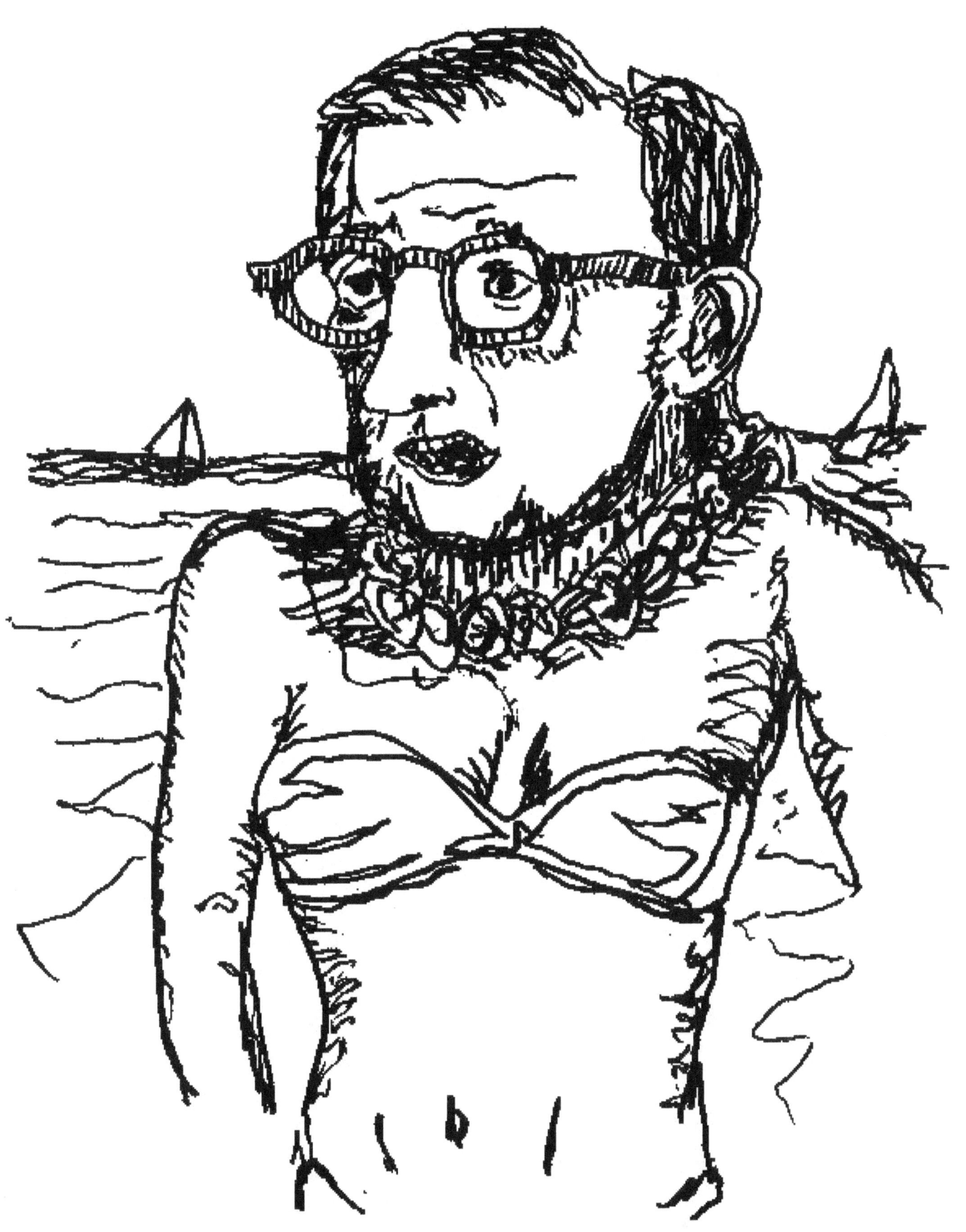

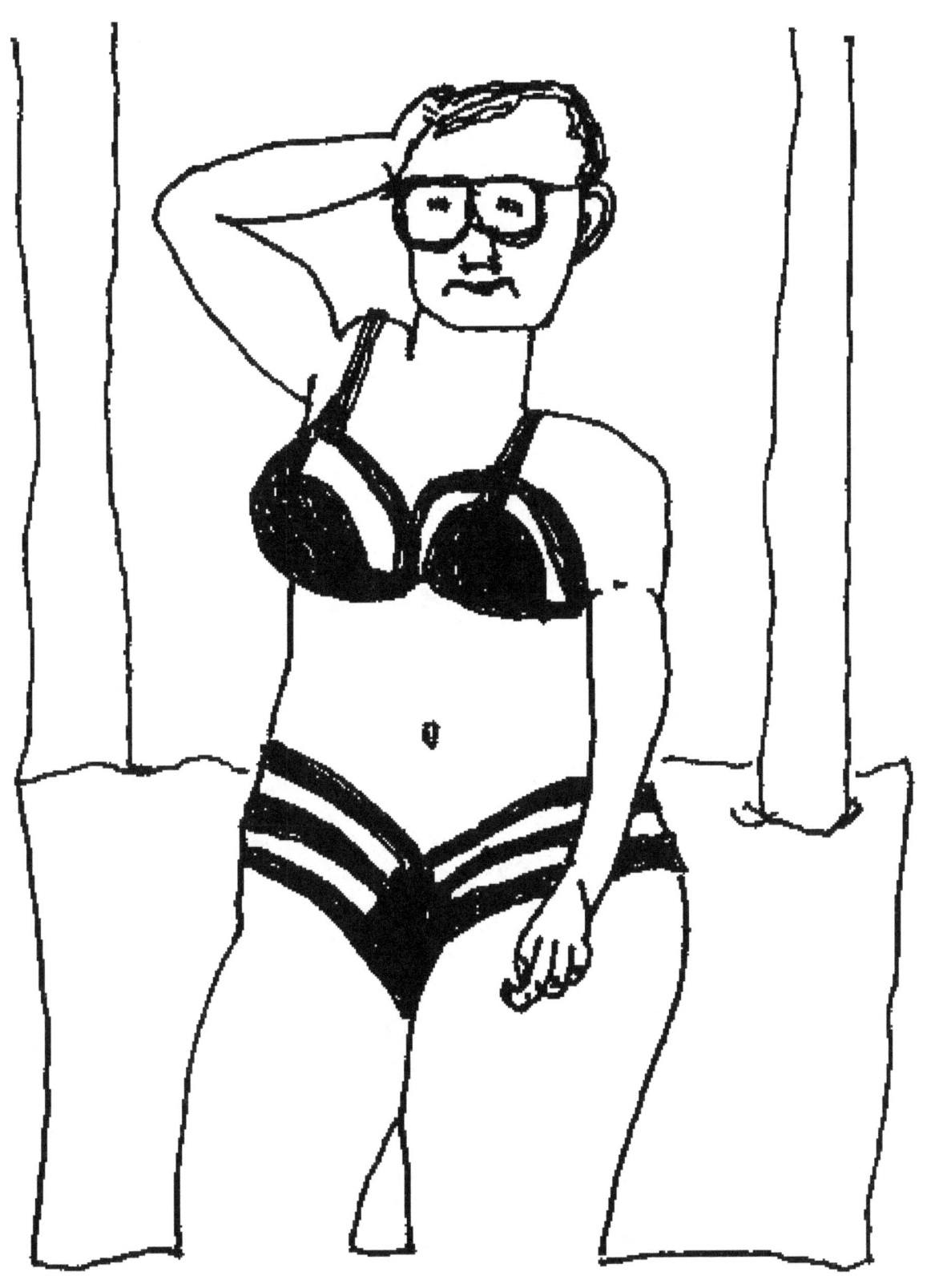

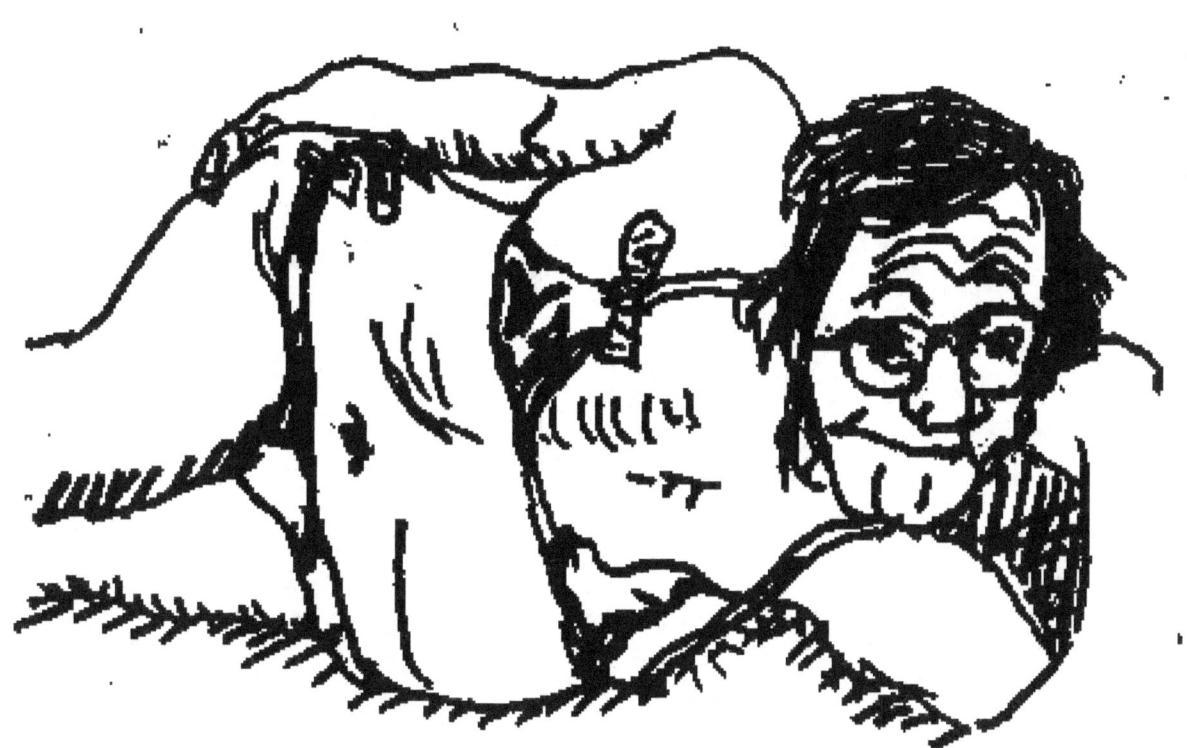

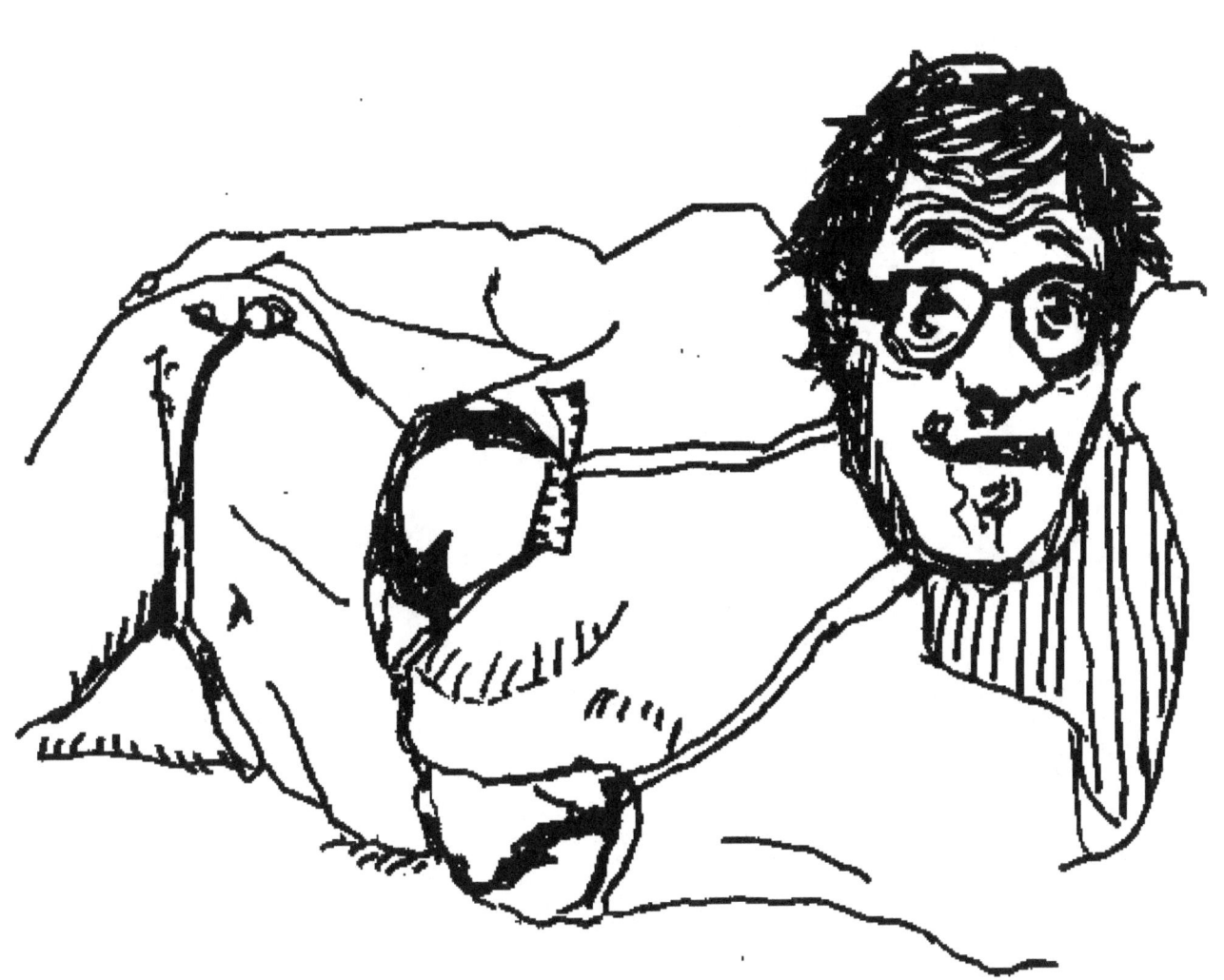

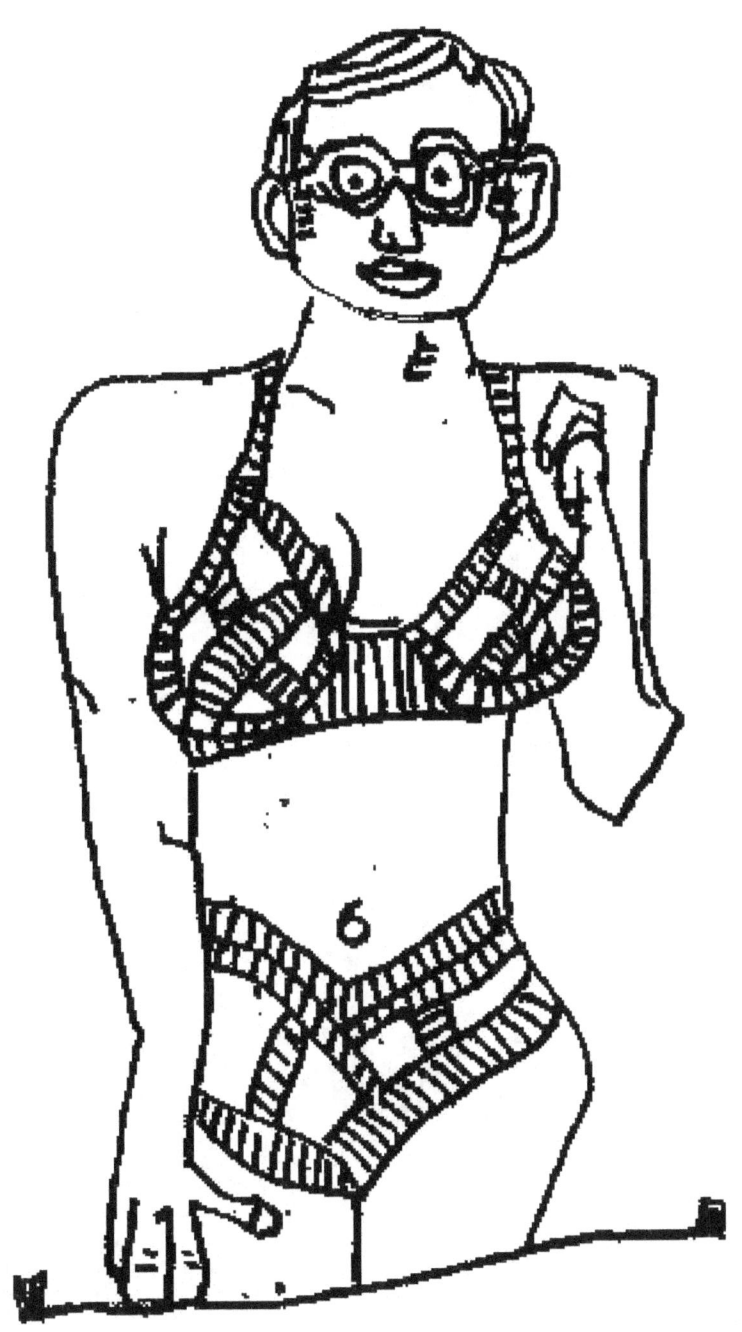

4.6.16
JOHN

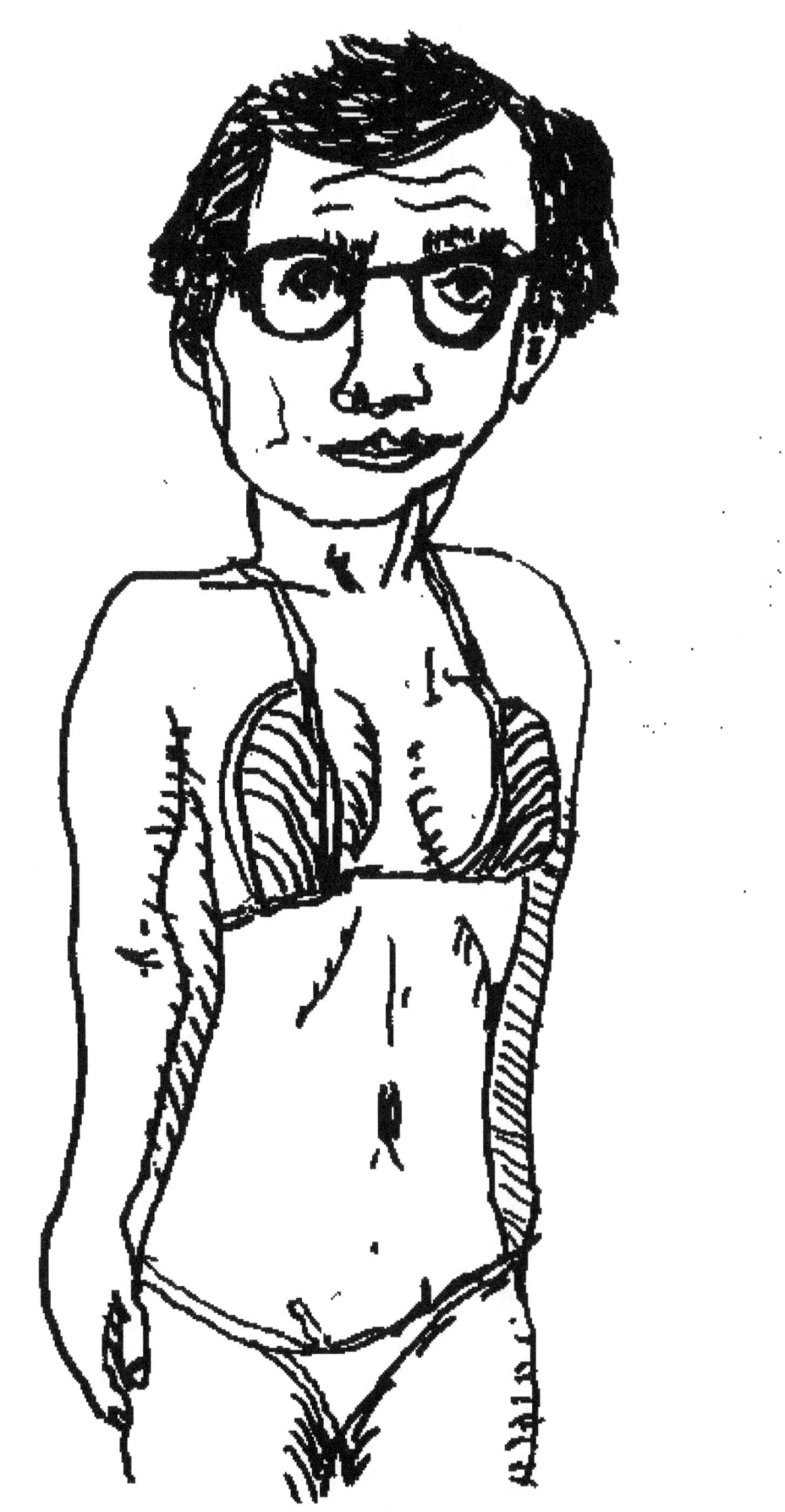

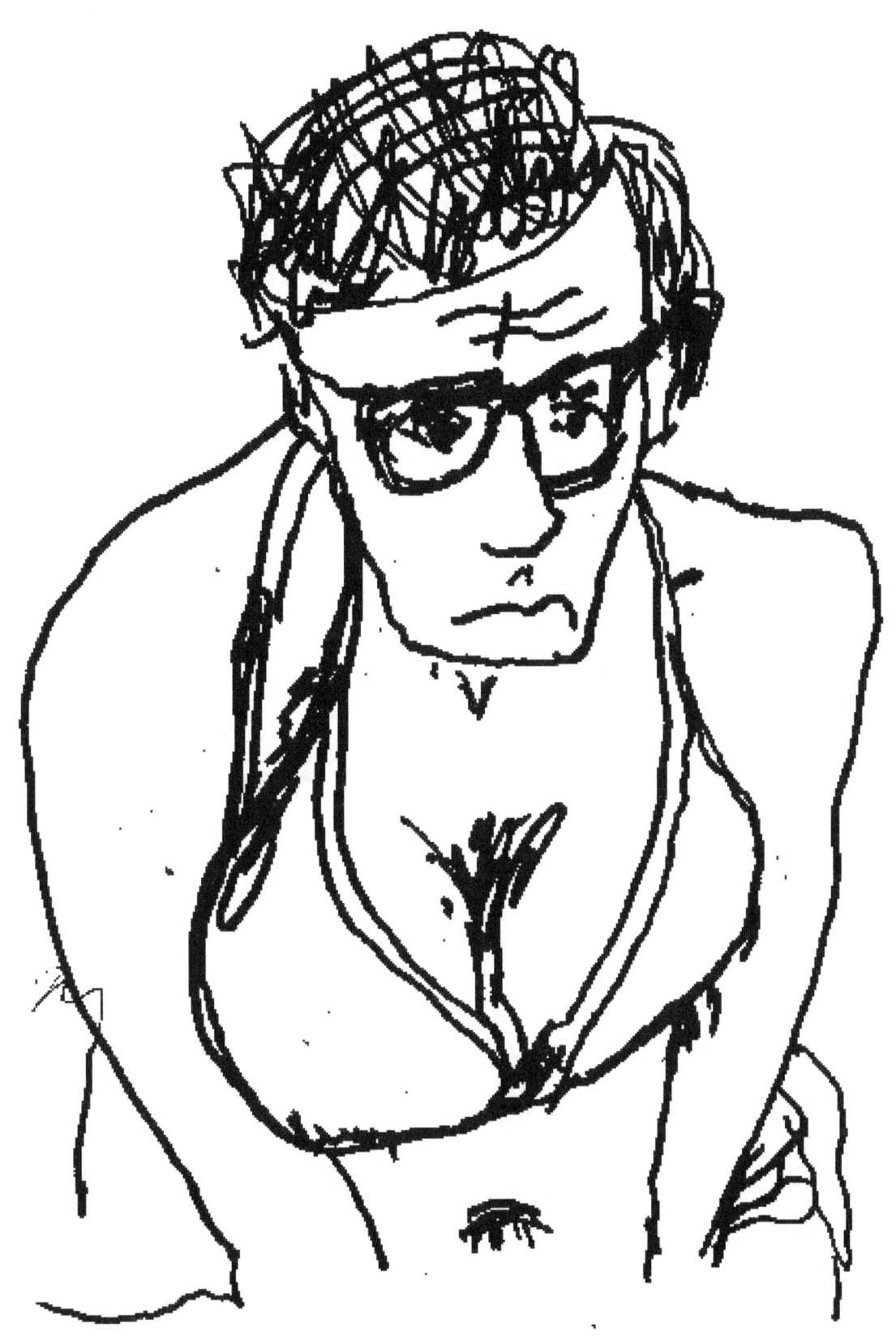

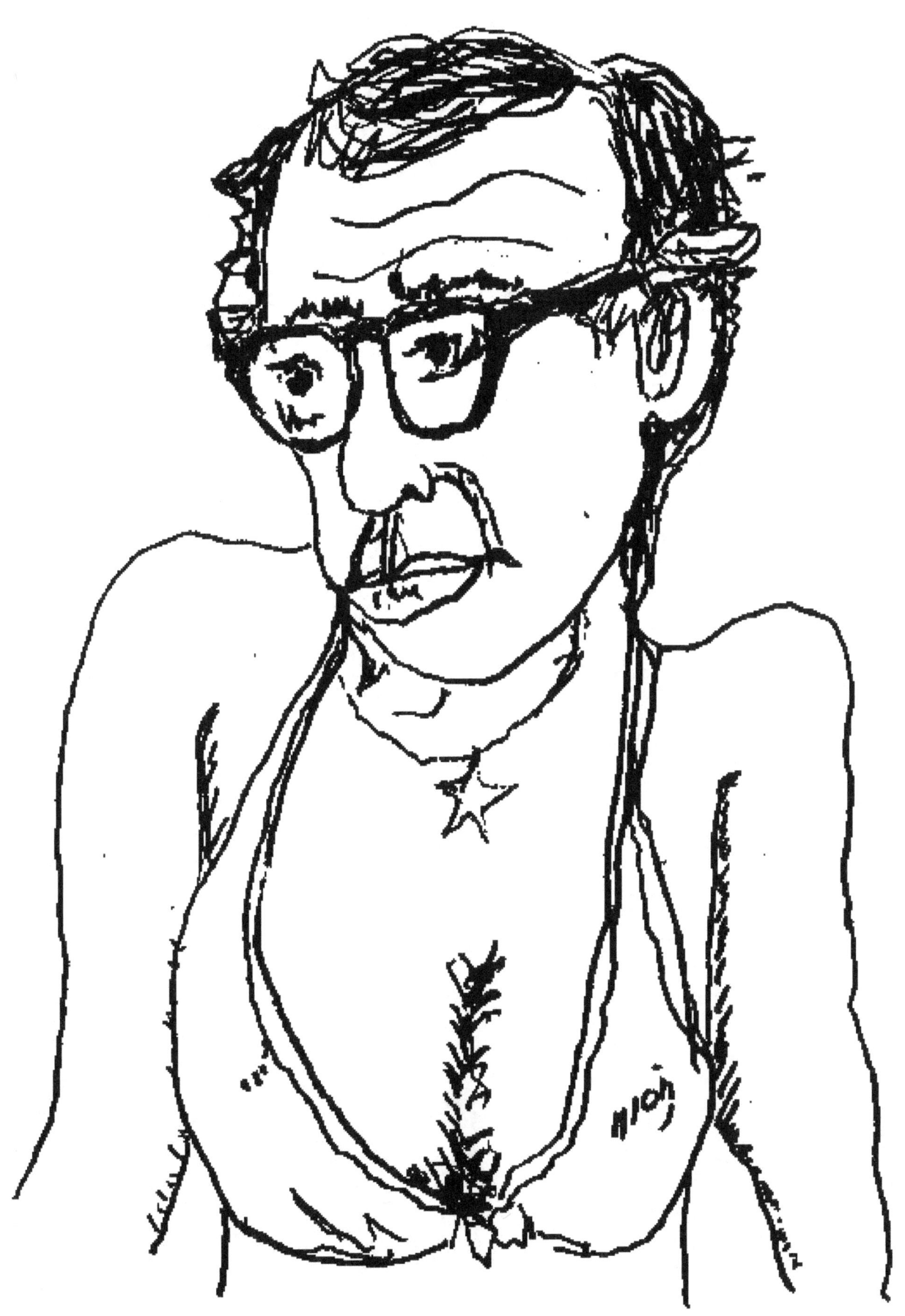

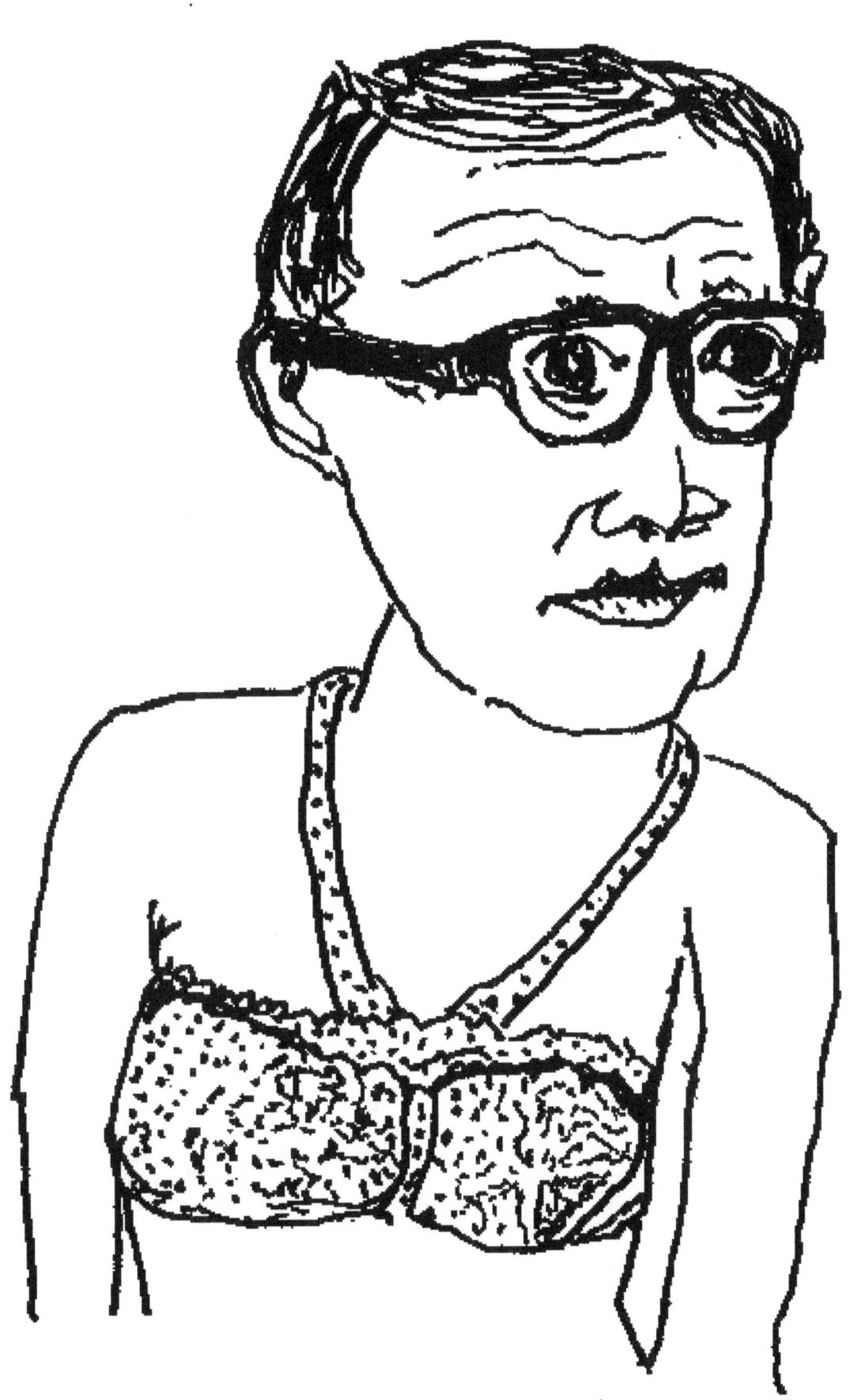

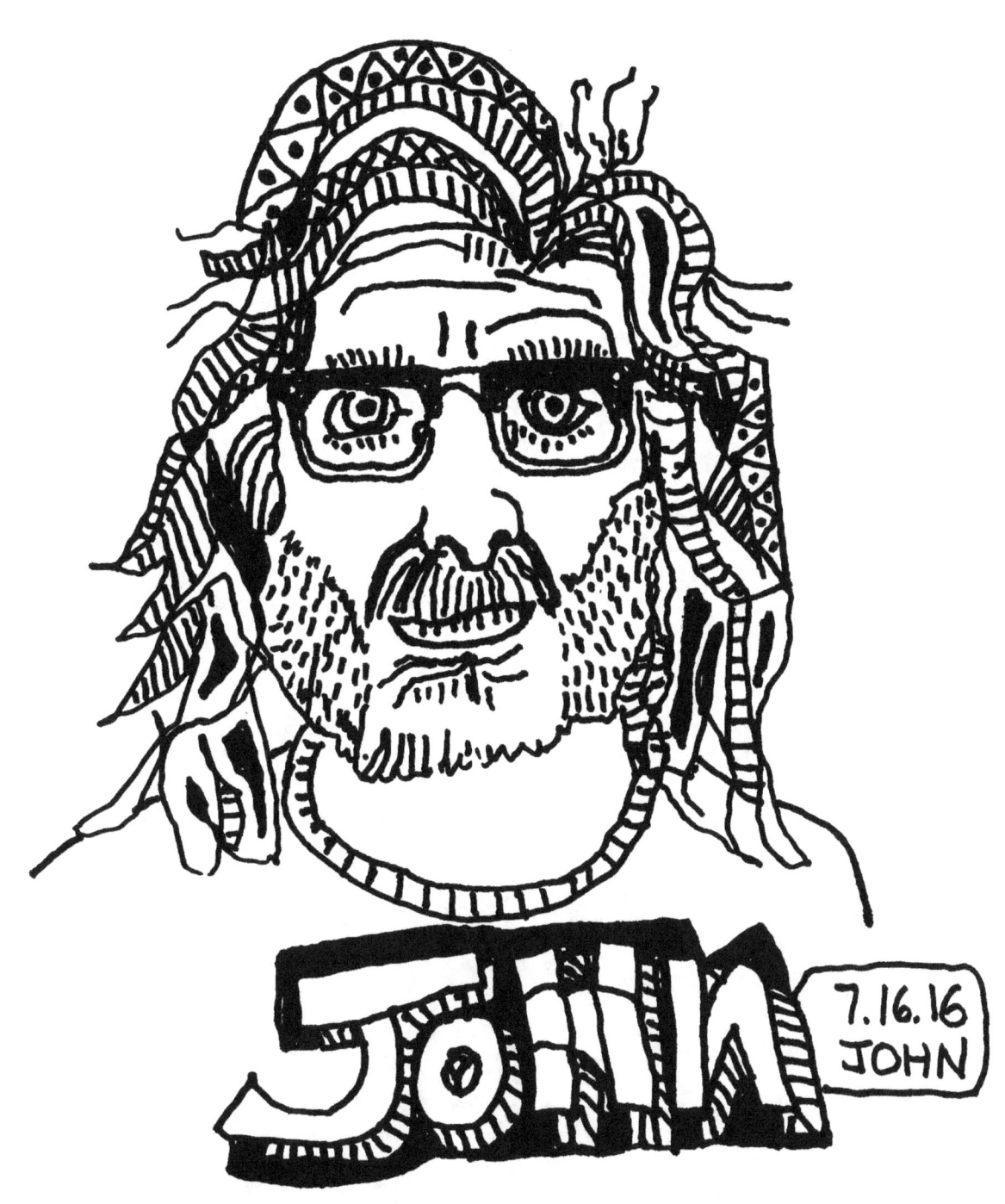

About the Author:

John Riegert lives in Pittsburgh, PA. He is an artist who
works in drawing and pretty much any medium. He is an OK guy.